52
WAYS
TO SHOW
AGING PARENTS
YOU CARE

➤➤52◀◀
WAYS
TO SHOW
AGING PARENTS
YOU CARE

Tracy Green
and
Todd Temple

A Division of Thomas Nelson Publishers

NASHVILLE

PUBLISHER'S NOTE: This book is intended for general
information only and is not intended to supplant advice by a
personal physician. Readers are urged to consult their parent's
personal physician before beginning any exercise or stretching
program for their parent.

Copyright © 1992 by Tracy Green and Todd Temple

Published in Nashville, Tennessee, by Oliver-Nelson Books, a division of
Thomas Nelson, Inc., Publishers, and distributed in Canada by Lawson
Falle, Ltd., Cambridge, Ontario.

Printed in the United States of America.

Library of Congress Cataloging-in-Publication Data

Temple, Todd, 1958–
    52 Ways to show aging parents you care / Todd Temple & Tracy
Green.
        p.   cm.
    ISBN 0-8407-9604-8 (paperback)
    1. Aging parents—United States—Psychology.   2. Parent and adult
    child—United States.   3. Aging parents—United States—Family
    relationships.   I. Green, Tracy, 1961–   .   II. Title.   III. Title: Fifty-
    two ways to show aging parents you care.
HQ1063.6.T46   1992   91-29430
646.7′8—dc20   CIP

1 2 3 4 5 6 — 97 96 95 94 93 92

This book is dedicated
with love
to
our families

Contents

Acknowledgments

We would like to thank the following people for lending their time and expertise to our project: Spring Asher, Wicke Chambers, Darlene Barrington, Karin Green, Dee Massengale, Dr. Janet Page, Phyllis Shavin, Robyn Spizman, and William Travis, Sr.

Using the Ideas in This Book

Remember when you were growing up and your parents always told you to "just do the best you can"? Well, that's what this book is about. Because that's all your parents want from you now that they're getting older. They need you to just do the best you can.

We hope this book will inspire you to do that. Of course, it's hard to know where to begin. And chances are, your life is very busy. It's okay. This book is filled with simple ways to help you do your best for your mom or dad . . . or aunt or uncle or grandparent or neighbor! You'll find practical ideas and information that will help you understand the needs and feelings of older folks. Whether your parents are living at home or in a nursing home, across town or across the country, whether they're sugary sweet or just plain impossible—you can make a difference in their lives.

As you look through *52 Ways to Show Aging Parents You Care,* don't feel overwhelmed. It's not intended for you to use all 52 ideas. Take a look inside . . . see what you like . . . see what makes sense for your parent and you . . . and try what you can. Do the best you can. Whatever you are able to do will be wonderful because it's done out of love for your parent.

As you'll see, we've used *he* in some places, *she* in others. That's to avoid having to say *he/she* and *his/hers* all the time. Just about all the ideas work for either sex.

1 Add an Animal to Your Parent's Life

Hold a true friend with both your hands.
—Nigerian proverb

Whether it's a pet in her house or an animal that comes by for "visits" at her retirement or nursing home, the companionship an animal can bring to your parent is incredible. For example, holding an animal in her arms can lower her blood pressure. That's just the beginning of the basis of "Pet Therapy." Counselors have shown an animal can bring all or some of these benefits to an older person's life:

- Improved health
- Better sense of happiness
- Higher self-esteem
- Improved social behavior
- Connection to reality
- Sense of responsibility and importance to another life

Visiting Pets Many homes for the elderly have regular programs of animal "visits," usually involving 10 to 15 pets. The visits provide memories, something to talk about and something to look forward to. If your parent is living in a home that doesn't have an animal visitation program, talk to the activities director. If she says she doesn't know where to begin planning one, suggest a call to the local Humane Society.

Live-In Pets   Many older folks complain that nobody needs them. When they become responsible for a pet, they feel needed and important again. A pet can eliminate a lot of the loneliness. And with a loud purr or slurpy kiss, a pet gives unconditional love every day.

So what kind of pet for your parent? Well, of course you need to consult with her. Here are some possibilities.

Dogs. A dog can be a great excuse to get out and exercise. Big dogs are a bonus for security, but certain breeds need such frequent and vigorous exercise that they aren't usually a good choice for seniors. Small dogs in general, particularly poodle breeds, tend to be easier for older folks to keep. Take your parent to the Humane Society and let her choose her own dog.

Cats. Quiet kitty cats make good pets for older folks. Even if your parent has never been too crazy about cats, their peaceful personalities may draw your parent in. Some people worry that cats are a problem for older people because they tend to be underfoot. There's some truth to this. A bell around the cat's collar can help. Your parent should consider choosing a cat that can live indoors and an adult rather than a frisky and more destructive kitten.

Birds. Birds aren't much fun in the petting or fetching departments, but they're convenient—especially for renters. Canaries, parakeets, and cockatiels are inexpensive and easy to take care of.

Fish. Watching swimming fish can relieve tension. Fish are extremely low-maintenance pets, but you still may need to find someone (a grandchild?) to feed the fish and periodically clean the tank.

2 Get Clothes-Smart

Any man may be in good spirits and good temper when he's well-dressed.
—Charles Dickens

"Well-dressed" doesn't mean your parent needs to be wearing an evening gown to the A&P. But she should be able to take pride, and comfort, in her appearance. You can help with that and in turn boost her self-confidence.

New Clothes We all feel better when we look good. But before you buy your parent new clothes or decide with him which ones will make the move to a new home, remember his clothes need to be

- washable
- sturdy
- roomy
- easy on, like front button or zip
- nonpullovers
- no iron

For women in wheelchairs, remember that skirts tend to ride up. So if your mom prefers skirts, get them extra long for her.

Shoes Many older women insist on wearing heels because they don't feel properly dressed without them. This is a tough one! Vanity has no age limit. Your parent wants to look nice and dignified. Try to at least get her into very low, sturdy heels, and make a goal together to find safer but pretty shoes like dress shoes with only a tiny lift to the heel.

Physical therapists tell us shoes are extremely important for seniors. Your parent can easily fall from slippery worn-out soles or any problem in design or fit that makes his steps unsteady. *Super solution:* the new walking shoes you see sold everywhere. They come from several makers in white, tan, black, brown . . . so if your parent is opposed to wearing something that looks like a sneaker all the time, he'll have a choice.

Everyday Wear All the different jogging/workout suits in the stores are ideal for older people. They fit all the criteria we just talked about. And they look snazzy. However, some seniors think they look like pajamas. You might try giving your parent a suit that is fairly non-pj-like for starters. Once she wears it a few times and realizes how comfy, cozy, and easy care it is, she'll probably want more of the same.

Ties For an older gentleman who likes to wear ties but tends to get them into food and vice versa, buy a can of fabric protector. Treat his entire tie wardrobe for him. Also a simple-to-attach tie tack will help keep that tie out of the way for him.

3 Play the Question Game

But enough about me, . . . let's talk about you: *What do* you *think of me?*
—Anonymous

Your parent probably has a lifetime of stories you've never heard. Treat yourself to some of those tales—let *him* do the talking, and you do the listening. He'll love it.

Inquisitive Inquiry The Question Game is a fun and easy way to do this. Here's a list of questions to get you started.

- Who was your first best friend?
- What surprises you most about growing older?
- Can you tell me three things you remember about your grandparents?
- What did you do when you were young that got you in trouble with your folks?
- Which Christmas holds the best memories?
- What were you really good at in school?
- Where were you the first time you saw TV?
- When you were 12, what did you want to be?
- When *I* was 12, what did you think I would be?
- What do you think is really ridiculous about the modern world?

- What is really wonderful about the modern world?
- Where did you meet your spouse? What did you think at first?
- What's the scariest thing that ever happened to you?
- Did you think Jack Benny was funny?
- Before air-conditioning, how did you keep cool?
- Was there anything you dreamed of doing that never worked out?
- Was there anything you dreamed of doing that came true?
- What was the hardest part of raising children?
- What was the first car you ever drove?
- When you were 21, how much money did you make?
- Do you remember how you celebrated the end of World War I or World War II?
- Is there anything you've dramatically changed your opinion on in the last 50 years?
- What sport were you good at?
- What kind of dancing did you like to do?
- Which brother or sister did you tell your secrets to most often?
- Did you ever have a hero?
- Did you vote for FDR the fourth time?
- Who's the most famous person you ever got to see in person?
- Did you ever see an Abbott and Costello film in the theater?

- If you could go to college now, what would you study?

You'll come up with dozens of great questions of your own once you get going. If you're really ambitious, keep a notebook every time you play the Question Game. You'll have a ready-made diary from your parent's life to read to the next generations.

4 Give Smart Gifts

When a father gives to his son, both laugh.
When a son gives to his father, both cry.
—Yiddish proverb

Aren't older folks the hardest people to buy gifts for? It seems like they either have everything or don't need anything! It may be true that there isn't much at the store you can find that would really be special to them. So forget the mall. They'll love these gifts that come directly from your heart.

Love Letter   Write a simple letter on the prettiest paper you can find, telling her all the things you love about her. Chances are, the last time you did this you were about 5 years old. And chances are, she's saved it all these years. How many gifts can you say that about?

Flowers   Instead of a flower arrangement from the florist, try these:

- Go to the gardening store for help in putting together a starter kit for a window box herb garden. This is a gift you can add to on other holidays, too.
- Bring a giant pot of red geraniums!

Top Five List   Have everybody in your family write down the top five favorite family memories. Put them all into a booklet with a family group picture on the cover.

Handy Box   Give her a brightly wrapped box full of things she needs all the time. Include stamps, stationery, a $10 long-distance phone call certificate, flashlights, tape, sponges, batteries, socks, panty hose, light bulbs, hair spray, soap, razors, toothbrushes, lotion, handkerchiefs, a large key ring, and combs.

Birthday Board   Paint all the family birthdays in bright colors on a wooden cutting board to be hung on the wall.

Christmas in July   No matter when her birthday is, wrap up several boxes of Christmas cards. When she opens them, offer to help her go through her address book, and address them all in time for the holidays.

Freeze Week   Freeze a week's worth of meals and put them in her freezer.

Freeze Time   Find a picture of your dad at about 6 years old, you at about 6, and your son at about 6. Have them all framed together. The styles may look different, but the smiles won't!

Carry-On Love Buy a plain canvas tote bag and fabric or acrylic "puffy" paints at the craft store. You can make your best effort at creating your own inspired design or get the little ones in on the act.

Give Back Wrap up his old fishing pole, and invite him to a picnic with you at the lake.

5 Find Your Parent a Roommate

Language has created the word "loneliness" to express the pain of being alone, and the word "solitude" to express the glory of being alone.
—Paul Tillich

Stories about loneliness don't usually have happy endings. But here's one that does, and it might inspire you if your parent lives alone.

Ernie is 71 years old. He lives near L.A. His marriage was a love affair that ended when his wife passed away last year. He misses her. He wants to keep living in his house; he has no interest in a retirement home, but for the first time in his life he is alone and lonely.

Here's the happy ending part. We found out about him when NBC's "Today" show featured him in a special story about seniors who decided to find roommates. Ernie went to Alternative Living for the Aging in Los Angeles, where they matched him up with another 71-year-old widower named Fred. Fred moved into Ernie's house. The setup took a little compromise—both men say they're set-in-their-ways kind of guys! But they say becoming roommates eased a lot of the loneliness out of their daily lives.

Roommate RX   Finding a roommate for your parent could ease the loneliness out of his daily life, too. Janet Witkin runs the organization that matched up Fred and Ernie. In fact, she's turned more than 3,000 seniors into roomies! She says older folks who move in with roomies often . . .

- laugh more.
- think of their aches and pains less.
- feel depressed less often.
- feel safer.
- find companionship.
- become more active.

There's no prescription in the world that can help your parent more than that! There are roommate match programs all over the country. In Atlanta, the Jewish Community Center provides Housemate Match. It's a program that matches up seniors and younger folks as roomies. The younger roommates are often students. The older housemates say they like having someone young around the house, someone to talk to, and in many cases someone they can cook for!

You might think your parent isn't a candidate for a roommate. That could be a matter of your own notion of what she wants. Ernie had the idea of the roommate on his own, but the folks at Housemate Match say it's often encouragement from family and friends that gets an older person to give serious thought to finding a roomie. The Agency on Aging in your state can find you an organization near you that works in this special area.

6 Simplify the Numbers

Our life is frittered away by detail. . . .
Simplify, simplify.
—Henry David Thoreau

Life is full of numbers. Phone numbers, area codes, bank accounts, PIN codes, addresses, ZIP codes, TV channels, appointment times. This numerical world is especially tough on an older person who suffers from memory loss or becomes disoriented occasionally. You can simplify things by putting important numbers on paper for him.

Wallet Numbers Type up an information card for his wallet and include . . .

- his name, address, and phone number
- Social Security number
- medical insurance—company and policy number
- physician's name and phone number
- your name and phone numbers

Phone Numbers Type or print in large letters a list of important telephone numbers, and place it next to the phone. If it's likely to be misplaced, laminate it and tape it to the countertop or nightstand. In addition to the information you put on the wallet card, you may want to include the phone numbers of other relatives, close friends, the pharmacist, and a cab company or senior transportation service.

Calendar Numbers With three brothers, four children, seven grandkids, and a great-grandchild, you can't expect him to remember birthdays. But you can remind him of these and other important dates by giving him a wall calendar with these dates already marked. Tape pictures of people to their birthdates.

TV Numbers Go through the TV listings together, and have him pick the shows he likes to watch each week. Then print the show names, times, and channel numbers in large type on a sheet of paper. Laminate the guide so it will survive use as a coffee table coaster. Make a new list every few months or so to keep up with program changes.

By the way, these last two ideas can be fun projects for a grandchild who likes art or knows how to do graphics on a computer.

7 Make the Phone Friendly

It was a delightful visit—perfect, in being much too short.
—Jane Austen

At the end of a telephone conversation, a Southerner might say, "It's been a pleasure visitin' with you." It's an interesting idea, *visiting* someone via phone line.

But for older people who live far from loved ones —or have a tough time getting out to see those close by—the telephone is their main means of visiting others. No need to dress up and drive across town (or deal with a delayed departure out of Dallas). It's just push a few buttons, and they're there.

To most older people, the telephone is a critical piece of equipment. So it makes sense that the right phone can make a great gift. Here are some shopping suggestions.

Jumbo Buttons A telephone with large buttons and easy-to-read numbers can be a big help to someone with bad eyesight or shaky hands. (However, a person with severe vision impairment may actually prefer a phone with the standard keypad because it's easier to operate by touch.)

No Cord Cordless phones are ideal for seniors who have a tough time getting around. There's no cord to trip over, and if they've brought the phone to where they're seated, no need to hurry across the room to answer it in time. Some cordless phones are so small they can fit in a vest pocket— these can be a lifesaver for someone who needs help but can't make it to a regular phone.

Speedy Dialing With family members moving farther apart and cities receiving new area codes, most of us have to dial 11 digits to call people we used to reach with 7. Speed dialing makes it easy to dial these long numbers and any other fre- quently called numbers.

Some phones have one-touch dialing—hit a but- ton marked "Doctor" and the phone automatically dials that number. With other phones you assign a two-digit code to each phone number—01 for the doctor, 02 for your office, etc. The most important feature is the one you don't think about until you plug it in: ease of programming. Some phones are simple to set up; others seem to require an engi- neering degree. If you want your parent to use this wonderful gift, plan on taking a half hour to set it up and show her how to operate it.

Help with Long Distance Some people wish their parents wouldn't call them so often. But if you have the opposite problem—a parent who doesn't call you *enough*—it may be the long-dis- tance bill that keeps her away. One company had just such a problem in mind when the company came up with the Call Me card: a calling card that allows the caller to call you and charge the call—

without having to make it "collect." Another company offers a personal 800 number that basically does the same thing, except the caller doesn't have to dial a calling card number to get through.

8 Make Things Readable

Of all the needs a book has, the chief need is that it be readable.
—Anthony Trollope

It's no wonder most adults enjoy reading children's books—they're filled with pictures and have big type. Those of us who write for grown-ups should take note of this. Instead, we use tiny type to cram hundreds of words onto each page.

Everything from check registers to water bills to the instructions for using a microwave oven is printed this way. If you have a parent with poor vision—nearsightedness, astigmatism, blurred vision, cataracts, or partial blindness—you can make his life more enjoyable with large type. Here's how.

Books Publishers release over 1,400 titles in large print each year. You can get large-print editions in many bookstores and libraries as well as directly from the publishers. These two publishers have mail-order programs for large-print books: Bantam, Doubleday & Dell Publishing, Inc., Large Print Program, 100 Pine Avenue, Holmes, PA 19043, (800) 345-8112; and G. K. Hall & Co., 100 Front Street, Riverside, NJ 08075-7500, (800) 257-5755.

For a comprehensive list of titles and publishers, look in the reference section of the library for *The*

Complete Directory of Large Print Books and Serials.
This annual directory also lists magazines and
newspapers available in large print.

Bibles are popular large-type books. Thomas
Nelson Publishers sells seven translations of the
Bible in large print.

Gifts   Look for items with easy-to-see instructions: telephones and microwaves with big key-
pads; clocks, thermometers, and radios with jumbo
displays; household appliances with controls la-
beled in large type.

Labels and Instructions   Use a label gun
(or white tape and a dark felt-tip pen) to relabel
appliances with hard-to-read type. Reprint instruc-
tion lists and booklets on an enlarging photo-
copier. Using large printing, write up your own
step-by-step instructions for things like operating
the telephone answering machine, adding a number to speed dial, or taping a TV show on the VCR
(that is, if you can figure out how to do it yourself!).

Addresses   Buy a large-print address book and
copy the contents of your parent's old book into it
using large block printing. While you're at it, up-
date the addresses and phone numbers.

9 Arrange a Rendezvous

Yes'm, old friends is always best, 'less you can catch a new one that's fit to make an old one out of.
—*Sarah Orne Jewett*

Life is like a loop. When you're a teenager, you have the time for lots of parties but don't have wheels (or permission) to get to them. When you're a grown-up, you have the wheels but little time. When you're older, you may find yourself back where you started—lots of time but no wheels.

If distance and travel difficulties have separated your parent from old friends, arrange a reunion.

Fly the Friend Let's say your dad's best childhood friend lives across the country where he and your father grew up. They correspond by letter but haven't seen each other for many years. Why not bring them together?

Contact your parent's friend; if he's able to travel, arrange the flight, pick him up at the airport, and let the two of them spend a weekend catching up on each other.

Fly Your Parent If your parent would like to do the traveling, make the arrangements for that to happen.

Host a Reunion Party   Maybe several of his friends live in the area but can't drive themselves to a get-together. Recruit other family members to chauffeur them to and from the party while you play host.

10 Ease the Flight Stress

To travel hopefully is a better thing than to arrive.
—*Robert Louis Stevenson*

The scariest part of flying isn't takeoffs or landings or turbulence. It's airport terminals. Ticket lines, hurried crowds, endless concourses, delayed departures, canceled flights, lost luggage—the pulse races just thinking about it all.

Here are some ways you can ease air travel trauma for an aging parent.

Make a Trip Card   Most people carry the itinerary in the ticket envelope, which isn't much help if they lose their tickets. You can avoid this problem and make his itinerary easier to read by printing his flight information on an index card in clear block letters. On the other side of the card write your phone number and that of the person picking him up. Also include a calling card number so he can reach you from any phone if there's a problem.

Carry the Drugs   Make sure your parent puts important medication in his carry-on luggage rather than in checked baggage. Lost luggage should be inconvenient, not life-threatening.

Team Up   The smoothest way to get an older person on a plane involves two people. The driver drops you off at the curb, checks the luggage, and finds a place to park. The escort walks with your parent, takes care of checking in, and gets him to the right gate.

Save Steps   At O'Hare Airport in Chicago, the distance from the curb to the farthest gate is one mile. To avoid a long and tiring airport hike for your parent, request a wheelchair or courtesy cart ride from the agent at the ticket counter. He can get the same service at his destination by telling a flight attendant on board the plane.

Board Early   Try to get to the gate 30 minutes before departure. Airlines usually allow seniors to board first so they can avoid the phone-booth-stuffing conditions that occur during general boarding.

Dine Well   Once on board, your parent is pretty much at the mercy of flight crew and fickle weather. The one exception is the food. Most airlines provide special low-sodium, low-cholesterol, kosher, or vegetarian meals to people who request them at least 24 hours in advance. (Ask what kinds of meals are available when you make your reservation.) These meals often taste better than standard fare because they're prepared by the dozens rather than by the thousands.

11 Take a Letter

Sir, more than kisses, letters mingle souls; for thus friends absent spark.
—*John Donne*

Once upon a time persons of high station seldom wrote their own letters. They left that inky job to clerks and secretaries. Maybe arthritis or eyesight problems have earned your parent this same privilege. Volunteer to be his secretary and let him dictate his letters to you.

When you've finished writing, let him sign the letter. Then take care of the rest—find the address, stamp the envelope, and mail it for him. Here are a few other things you can do as his correspondence secretary.

Pictures   Make several copies of a recent photo and include one with each letter.

Letterhead   If he's a big letter writer, order a set of personal stationery from the local print shop.

Correspondence Kit   Put together a box with stamps, paper, and envelopes. Stamp and address a few envelopes to people he writes frequently.

Voice Letter If he lives far away, you can still help him send letters. Give him an inexpensive cassette recorder, some blank cassettes, and a few stamped and addressed shipping envelopes. He can dictate into the recorder and send his voice letters directly to friends and family.

12 Send a Book on Tape

Reading is to the mind what exercise is to the body.
—Sir Richard Steele

The oldest generation of Americans grew up without TVs, VCRs, CNN, or "20/20." For information and entertainment, they relied upon books, newspapers, radio, and what they overheard at the barbershop or beauty parlor. Theirs was an age of words—written and spoken—not pictures.

If your parent is visually impaired he's cut off from many of these words—reading becomes difficult or impossible. But thanks to audiocassettes, he can read with his ears.

Even older people with perfect vision enjoy audio programs. They grew up in the big days of radio and are accustomed to learning and laughing through listening. Here are a few audio gifts your parent may appreciate.

Audio Books Bookstores carry condensed versions of many popular books on audiocassette. For complete books, look for a tape rental library. Books on Tape, Inc., carries over 3,000 titles you can order by phone and have sent to you for a 30-day period. Each set of tapes comes in its own postage-paid return box; when you've finished the book, you just drop the package in the mail.

Each book is recorded by a professional "reader" whose voice characterizations make the book interesting to listen to. Contact the company if you'd like to receive a catalog of titles: Books on Tape, Inc., P.O. Box 7900, Newport Beach, CA 92658, (800) 626-3333.

Bible on Tape   Several publishers offer different versions of the Bible on audiocassette. For example, Thomas Nelson Publishers offers a fourteen-cassette audio New Testament in the New King James Version narrated by Johnny Cash.

Retro Radio   Many of the great radio dramas, comedies, and variety shows of the thirties, forties, and fifties have been recorded onto cassette. You may be able to find some of these tapes at a book or record store. Wireless, a mail-order company specializing in radio show–related products, sells collections of old radio shows by Jack Benny, Amos 'n' Andy, Red Skelton, and others. To ask for a catalog, contact Wireless, P.O. Box 64422, Saint Paul, MN 55164-0422, (800) 669-9999.

Live to Tape   If you're attending a live lecture, sermon, or concert, tape the program with a portable cassette recorder, and send the tape to your parent. Some events don't allow you to make your own recording, but that's usually because they're selling tapes. As a service to shut-ins, some churches will send a sermon tape every week to those on their list.

13 Connect the Generations

*Everyone has been a child. All can
understand through muffled memory
how childhood was. But none has been
old except those who are that now.*
—Bert Kruger Smith

Today's children are growing up with few roots.
Compared to your kids, you probably spent much
more time with grandparents, aunts, and uncles.
These relatives helped you understand who you
were and where you came from. Busier lives and
smaller and more spread-out families prevent
many of today's children from connecting with
their heritage.

That's the bad news. The good news is that you
can do something about these problems *and* show
love to your parent by bringing three or more generations together.

Hand-Me-Down Cooking It's hard to believe that humans survived for thousands of years
without benefit of cookbooks. Each generation
handed down cooking knowledge to the next—the
family traditions and cultural heritage went along
for the ride. Make sure this process doesn't stop
now. Invite your parent to be master chef and your
children his protégés. Prepare and serve an old
family recipe.

Traditions   Family traditions help bind generations together—they remain the same while everything around us is changing. Hold onto holiday traditions. For example, ask your parent to help you
re-create some of the Christmas traditions he remembers from his own childhood. Where there is
no tradition, start one.

Namesakes   At a family gathering ask your
parent to tell everyone who *his* parents were
named after—and how his own name was chosen.
Then let him explain how the names for you and
your siblings were picked. You can describe the
reasons behind the names of your children. Ask
your kids to think of what they'd like to name their
own children and why.

Story Time   Ask your parent to tell your kids a
story he remembers hearing from his own parents
or grandparents. If it's a good one, ask him to tell it
again on another occasion. At the next gathering,
let one of your children tell the same story while
granddad listens.

Three-Story Views   Ask a question and let
each generation answer it. For example, ask everyone to describe his elementary school. This gives
Gramps another opportunity to lengthen the distance and increase the depth of snow he trudged
through to get to school; you can talk about how
girls were sent home for wearing pants; and your

daughter can describe the computers she used in kindergarten. Talk about the similarities, too.

Other three-story topics include most embarrassing moment, what you wanted to be when you grew up, earliest memory, favorite song, best friend, first job, and best vacation.

Visit His Childhood   If possible, take a family trip to where your parent grew up. A walk down memory lane will be fun for him—and it will give your children a sense of their heritage.

14 Shoot a Video

History is a pact between the dead, the living, and the yet unborn.
—*Edmund Burke*

Home video makes it possible for grandchildren and great-grandchildren and other descendants yet unborn to meet your aging parent. To help your family get to know him better now—and to remember him when he's gone—conduct a personal interview in front of your video camera.

Interview Tips *Comfortable.* Choose a setting where he'll feel at ease—sitting in his favorite living room chair or at the kitchen table or lounging in the yard.

Casual. Talking to a camera is awkward. Set up the interview so he can speak to you without having to stare into the lens. To do this, imagine that his chair is in the center of a clock face. Set the camera on a tripod at the six o'clock position facing him, and place your chair between the four o'clock and five o'clock positions.

He's the Star. Zoom in on him from the waist up. There's no need for you to be in the picture—you'll get your chance when your children record *your* video (in 3-D, probably).

Conversational. Prepare a list of questions you intend to ask. Go over them together before the interview, and let him add or remove questions from the list. However, use the questions more as a rough guide to the conversation than as a checklist that must be completed.

Real Life. If you sneeze or he misses a question or a grandchild runs naked through the picture, just keep the camera rolling. Give family members a glimpse of what your parent is like in real life.

Make several copies of the interview to give to other family members. By the way, if you don't have a video camera, record the interview on audiotape instead.

Family Camera   There are other ways a video camera can help your parent feel a part of the family. Send him a tape of a grandchild's birthday party, music recital, or soccer game. If you can't be with him on his birthday, tape a greeting of your kids singing "Happy Birthday."

If your parent has a difficult time remembering the names of his grandchildren (and sons-in-law!), put together a video picture album. Have family members introduce themselves on camera—name, age, hobbies, favorite food. He'll really appreciate this video if he gets it a week or so before a family get-together so he can practice putting names to faces.

15 Call Your Mom

Reach out.
—AT&T commercial

Pick up the phone. It's the simplest thing you can do to show your parent you care. But what do you say when she answers? Try one of these.

"I Love You"   A short call.

"I Need Your Help"   There's nothing like being needed. Ask for her opinion on something; seek her advice on a decision you're making; ask her how to keep the crust from burning in her cheesecake recipe.

"You're a Great Mom"   Her age may prevent her from doing many of the things she used to do, but she can still be your mom. Let her know she's still good at it.

"Do You Remember When . . . ?"   Remind her of a moment when she taught you an important lesson. She'll be thrilled to know that moment still matters to you.

16 Lend a Hand

To look up and not down,
To look forward and not back,
To look out and not in, and
To lend a hand.
—*Edward Everett Hale*

Many older folks who live on their own have a tough time keeping up with the dozens of cleaning, repairing, and home improvement jobs that are a part of any household. Drop in and lend a hand with vacuuming, cleaning, dusting, washing, or ironing. Here are more working gestures that your parent will appreciate.

High Dust Many seniors have no business climbing on ladders or standing in chairs to reach dust on high surfaces. So, you dust these places. Also look for shelves covered with bric-a-brac and other hard-to-dust areas.

Proper Places Bring order to a corner of the house that needs organizing—a closet, desk drawer, file cabinet, kitchen cupboard, medicine chest.

New Year Checkup At the beginning of the year help your parent sort and file the financial and medical records, loose photographs, correspondence, and anything else that's been neglected during the past year.

Throw a Work Party   Get the family to pitch in for an all-day house cleanup and fix-up party in the Amish barn-building tradition. Paint a room, mend the porch, clean up the yard, chop firewood, hang wallpaper, fix a leak, unsqueak a door. Send out a scout beforehand to find out what work your parent wants done and what kinds of tools and equipment you'll need. Plan the work to keep everyone busy—and out of each other's way. And don't forget to assign someone to refreshments.

17 Give to the Cause

Freely ye have received. Freely give.
—Jesus

You can show older people you care about their lives by contributing to agencies that serve them.

Give Locally Adult day-care programs, home-delivered meals services, and other needed programs for older adults are usually run by nonprofit organizations in the local area. That means they rely upon contributions—from government, foundations, corporations, and individuals—to keep their vital programs alive. Identify the groups serving aging adults in your parent's community, and support them with your gifts.

The easiest way to find out who's serving seniors is to contact the Area Agency on Aging office in your community or county. It has a complete listing of organizations and how to reach them. (If your parent lives elsewhere, your local office can give you the phone number of the agency in your parent's community.)

Fund the Fight If your parent is suffering from a chronic health problem such as cancer, diabetes, or arthritis, give money to an organization dedicated to fighting that ailment. For example, if your mom suffers from heart disease, contribute money to the American Heart Association in tribute to her. The association will send *you* a receipt for your donation and send *her* a card that acknowledges your tribute and contains a personal greeting from you to her.

Other national health foundations have similar tribute programs—your local chapter can tell you what's available.

Dedicate Your Work   Authors and singers aren't the only ones allowed to dedicate their work to someone they love. For example, your daughter can dedicate an evening of baby-sitting to an arthritic grandparent. She calls her grandmother: "Granny, I'm dedicating my work on Friday night to you. Whatever money I earn I'm going to send to the Arthritis Foundation to help them find a cure." Work is more fulfilling when it's a labor of love.

18 Write a Poem

How do I love thee? Let me count the ways.
—Elizabeth Barrett Browning
in a sonnet to Robert Browning

Memories, wishes, love—these are the only tools a person needs to have the perspective of a poet! Even if neither you nor your parent has ever written a poem, this can be a powerful inspiration to share. We promise it's easier than you think.

The Instant Poem Kit Write the word *YOU* at the top and bottom of a piece of paper. In between, just list any words at all that come to mind when you think of your parent: images, colors, moments, emotions. Don't even think about rhyme or rhythm—there is absolutely no such thing as doing this wrong. Check out this example:

> YOU
> huggable
> lovable
> lullaby singer
> cookie baker
> beautiful
> glorious
> YOU

See? Maybe it's not a masterpiece, but it's pure poetry to the ears of the person it's written to. You and your parent can try this Starter Poem with each other. Or you can write a Starter Poem to her on your own. The perfect title? Just "Mom."

Here's one written from a daughter to her father for his birthday, built from a simple Starter Poem.

"Happy Birthday, Dad"

YOU.
Dad.
Man-in-the-moon cheese grin.
Eyes that look so much like mine.
The good-night tuck-in man.
The Ultimate Cubs Fan.

A little grey?
Okay.

You smiling
swirling
shining star.
You.

A poem is a very personal thing to share. Writing is a positive way to deal with feelings. It helps us all to let the feelings out, process them, and look over them on paper. Your parent might like to try writing a poem about the grandchildren, her pets, her house, a memory—anything.

19 Mail a Party

The manner of giving is worth more than the gift.
—Pierre Corneille

If you can't be there for a parent's birthday, send a party in the mail instead. For a traditional birthday party-in-a-box, make sure you pack the essentials.

Decorations

- Confetti
- Streamers
- Balloons (use very small balloons or a very large box)
- Silly hat

Entertainment

- Party horns
- Those things that unravel like a chameleon's tongue
- Yo-yo, marbles, or jacks

Refreshments

- Birthday cookies
- Cupcake with candle (unlit)

- Ice cream (freeze-dried)
- Package of flavored drink mix

You really don't have to wait around for a birthday to mail a party. Any special occasion—or no occasion at all—can justify a party package. Send a Happy New Year celebration box, an Easter egg hunt-by-mail, a Fourth of July box party, or a Halloween trick-or-treat package.

20 Play Games

The mind ought sometimes to be diverted, that it may better return to thinking.
—*Phaedrus*

Remember parlor games? Your parent probably remembers playing them. Families and friends would sit together to play games, talk, eat, argue about the rules, and laugh. TVs and VCRs have taken over our parlors now. But games can be a blast.*

Games are big with the older set. A good afternoon of playing with friends will stimulate your parent's mind, memory, and competitive juices and help get her together with folks her own age.

Board Games The business world has already figured out that board games for seniors are BIG BUSINESS. You'll have no trouble finding grown-up games at the store.

Scrabble. This is the most popular board game with seniors. (Bridge is the most popular game overall.)

Trivial Pursuit, The Vintage Years. This version of the game covers the time between Lindbergh's

---

* Some info for this chapter came from the article in the Atlanta *Journal Constitution,* April 17, 1991, by staff writer Frances Cawthon.

1927 flight and the end of Eisenhower's presidency in 1961.

Balderdash. Based on the old parlor game called Dictionary, where each player had to find some bizarre or obscure word in the dictionary and either come up with the right definition or bluff everybody into believing a bogus definition, Balderdash comes with large, neatly printed cards.

Pictionary. Each player has a minute to draw clues about a word or phrase. Do your parent a thoughtful favor and buy the party edition because it comes with a drawing easel that's easy to use and see instead of the tiny notepad in the regular edition.

Senior Series. Poker-Keeno, Tripoley, Bingo, and Rumi K have versions with large-print cards, dice, and score pads, and the special dice are designed to cut down on the noise level.

Playing Cards   Make sure your parent has large-print playing cards around the house. That way she can always have a deck on hand for Bridge with friends or Fish with the grandkids.

TV Game Shows   If your parent absolutely insists on watching the TV game shows that so many older folks are crazy about, better to join her than to argue with her about it. You can team up together to beat the TV contestants and keep a tally of how much cash you could have won together if you were the ones at the TV studios.

21 Check the Lights

Fire is seen in the eyes of the young, but it is light that we see in the old man's eyes.
—*Victor Hugo*

Here's an important fact: Older people need about three times as much light as younger people to see clearly and avoid falling.

You can help by making some simple adjustments to the lighting in your parent's house or room. Some of them might raise the light bill slightly . . . so expect your parent to object if he's taken pride in a lifetime of low light bills! None of the following ideas will increase a light bill substantially. They'll simply make things safer.

More Watts Increase the wattage in every lamp and overhead light fixture in his house or room. If it's 60 watts now, put in 100 watt bulbs wherever possible. This is a particularly big help anywhere that your dad normally reads and in staircases and hallways that may have been shadowy for years.

More Lights Walk through his house in both daytime and nighttime and check that there are lamps near every chair and near the bed. Make sure that the top and bottom of every staircase has a bright light.

Another idea: Night-lights in every socket between his room and the bathroom can light the way better for that much-traveled path.

Bulbs and Tubes   For general room lighting, go with fluorescent tubes wherever you can. They don't have much glare. They're also economical, of course. For reading and work areas, regular incandescent light bulbs have the best contrast and a nice clear beam.

Glare   Glare from sun coming in the house can momentarily blind your parent and cause a fall. You don't want to keep out all the glorious sunshine, but make sure every window has a venetian blind or window shade on it that your parent can easily reach and work without help.

Sunglasses   Sunglasses will be a cool fashion move for your parent, and they're a smart idea year-round. Glare from the sun can cause a fall in January as well as August. And of course they'll help protect his eyes from the damage of those ultraviolet rays. Make sure he gets new prescription sunglasses every time his regular eyeglass prescription is changed. If you can't find a two-for-one deal, he can try clip-on shades.

22 Be Sensitive to the Senses

What is the secret of the trick?
How did I get so old so quick?
—Ogden Nash

The aging process does a lot more than gray the hair, wrinkle the skin, and slow the driving. Growing older has a big effect on the senses—and with it, a person's perception of the world. By knowing about some of these sensory changes, you can better understand how to care for your parent.

Vision Muscles and joints aren't the only things that stiffen with age. The eye's lens loses its elasticity, too, making it difficult to focus on close objects or small print. This condition, called presbyopia, becomes noticeable to people in their thirties and forties and grows worse from there. Without prescriptive lenses, a person in her sixties or seventies may not be able to read.

Hearing Older adults often lose the ability to hear high-pitched sounds because the sensory receptors that pick up these frequencies become damaged over time.

Another problem is that speech loses its crispness and clarity. This makes it difficult to distinguish between similar-sounding words or to isolate a conversation from background noise. You can minimize the confusion by speaking directly at the person so she can synchronize the proper sounds to your lips and by limiting background noise from TVs, stereos, other conversations, and shouting grandkids.

Smell Up to half of those 65 and older have a major smell dysfunction. While the inability to smell certain things could be considered a blessing, it also means the person is less likely to detect leaking gas, smoke, toxic fumes, or spoiled food. She might also tend to use too much perfume—the olfactory equivalent of someone talking with headphones on.

A person with diminished sense of smell misses out on many of the sweet smells of life—and the memories triggered by them. Also, food doesn't taste as good because smell and taste are closely related.

Taste Except for losses related to smell, the sense of taste stays pretty strong as a person ages. However, it becomes less consistent—the same food can taste different from one day to the next. A person with a full set of upper dentures may think that food is more bland because sensors in the roof of the mouth are obstructed.

Touch The other senses may come and go, but touch was the first to comfort us and it stays true to the end. Touching is important to every human;

to an aging parent with other impaired senses, it is critical. Stay in touch with hugs and kisses, hand-shakes and handholds, back rubs and neck massages.

23 Set Up a Job

When people are serving, life is no longer meaningless.
—John Gardner

With the number of service jobs growing—and fewer teenagers to fill those jobs—many employers have been asking seniors to "unretire." That's why you see more older adults behind sales, fast-food, and checkout counters.

These aren't all high-paying jobs, but then again, paychecks aren't everything. For lots of older workers the real payoff is in working with others and knowing that they can still be productive.

Good Service Restaurants, retail stores, hotels, and other service businesses have gotten serious about seniors. National chains like McDonald's have started special programs to recruit and train older adults.

If your parent is healthy, active, and outgoing, he may enjoy a part-time position where he can chat with customers, be a role model for younger workers, and earn a little spending money for spoiling the grandkids.

Old Pro Owners of small or new businesses often need outside help with bookkeeping, taxes, sales training, or business organization but can't afford the hourly fees of professionals. Your parent may be skilled in areas that can help a growing business.

Ask among your friends and associates to see if anyone can use what your parent can offer. A classified ad or bulletin board notice can also bring in business.

24 Volunteer 'Em

No one is useless in this world who lightens the burdens of another.
—*Charles Dickens*

From the mailroom to the boardroom, nonprofit agencies thrive on volunteers. If your parent is active and eager to work, someone in his community is waiting for his call. Here are a few organizations that need him:

- Hospitals—gift shop, reception, helping patients
- Schools—office help, teacher assistants
- Churches and synagogues—mailings, child care, teaching, maintenance, housekeeping, help for shut-ins
- Community theaters—support mailings, ushering, set construction, costume making
- Day-care centers—meals, crafts, working with children
- Local chapters of national organizations such as the Red Cross and the American Cancer Society—mailings, office work, fund-raising, teaching

Work for Free. There's no rule that says volunteers must work for a nonprofit. If your business does large in-house mailings of invoices, newsletters, or advertisements, ask your parent and a few of his friends to fold, stuff, seal, stamp, and sort. You'll get a tedious job done for the cost of a snack; they'll get an opportunity to shoot the breeze while they work. Other tasks for office volunteers include answering the phone, processing product information requests, filing, addressing invitations, and assembling information packets, press kits, reports, and notebooks.

If you use senior volunteers, express your appreciation by making the experience enjoyable.

- Team up. Look for tasks that involve two or more people.
- Provide rides. Arrange transportation to and from your office.
- Play host. Introduce them to coworkers; make them feel at home.
- Make it short. Keep the task to four hours or less with time for breaks.
- Serve a snack. Provide refreshments.
- Say thanks. Let them know how much you appreciate their work.

25 Sign 'Em Up

Messenger of sympathy and love, servant of parted friends, consoler of the lonely, bond of the scattered family, enlarger of the common life.
—Inscription
Post Office in Washington, D.C.

Thanks to the growing population of older people, the number of facilities and agencies dedicated to serving them is also growing: retirement communities, senior clubs and centers, adult day-care and health centers, meal programs, and so on.

What's more, lots of existing organizations are starting or expanding their programs for senior adults—hospitals, city parks departments, schools, churches, community centers, health clubs, YMCAs, Red Cross chapters, and the local chapters of national health organizations such as the American Cancer Society and the American Diabetes Foundation.

To find out who offers services to older people in your parent's community, contact the area Agency on Aging for that community. Ask for a directory.

Mailing Lists Once you have the directory, you can contact individual organizations and ask them to put your parent on the mailing list. This guarantees that your parent will hear about health screenings, special events, and new programs being offered in the community. Sign her up to receive the senior newsletter and mailings from these organizations.

- Hospitals may offer health fairs; free screenings for foot problems, cholesterol, or glaucoma; and volunteer opportunities.
- Senior clubs and community centers offer excursions, concerts, special events, workshops, seminars, lectures, and information on health services and employment.
- Local chapters of the Red Cross and American Heart Association offer free health screenings, seminars, and volunteer opportunities.

AARP Another organization she may appreciate hearing from is the American Association of Retired Persons. A one-year membership to the AARP is only $5. The member gets 6 issues of *Modern Maturity* magazine and some discounts on things such as hotels and rental cars. For a membership application, contact AARP, 1909 K Street NW, Washington, DC 20049, (202) 872-4700.

26 Knock Down Walls

An old man loved is winter with flowers.
—German proverb

If your relationship with your aging parent isn't exactly perfect, you're hardly alone. Difficult memories, painful emotions, and walls created over the years are hard to just forget about and put aside. Maybe it's hard for you to talk openly, to hug without awkwardness.

Atlanta psychotherapist Dr. Janet Page says there are four common emotions that create walls between adult children and their aging parents.

Guilt The Big *G*—GUILT—hits children of aging parents hard. But it doesn't have to keep you down or come between you and your parent while you still have him here with you.

Well, it's never too late for honesty. Tell your parent where you think you've failed as a child. You're probably thinking, *Oh, I could never do that.* But you can. It can change your life and your relationship with your parent. Say, "Dad, I love you. I feel like I haven't done enough. I'm sorry I (fill in the blank). I'm sorry I never (fill in the blank). I would change it all if I could." No one in your life will love you like your parent does. He probably forgave you long before you could ever forgive yourself. He may have had a totally different view of the situations you're torturing yourself over. The part of the talk that will mean the most to him is the part where you say, "I love you."

Even if your parent is ill or confused, do your best to have some form of this conversation. Seal it with a hug. It will heal you both in your hearts.

Fear Just about everybody is afraid to talk about death. Maybe your parent has tried to bring up the topic, but you've put him off. If it's hard for you to know what to say when your parent wants to talk about dying, give yourself a break and don't say anything. Let him talk.

If he is sick, if he has lost close friends, death is probably on his mind. Let him get it out. If it makes you cry, then cry. Hug. Let him know you'll miss him and you love him.

Anger This one is really hard to admit: *How can I be angry at this older man?* Maybe you're mad at your parent for one thing, or maybe for a lifetime of things. And now that he's older, you still can't seem to let go of it. But you'll always have a wall between the two of you if you don't.

It might be an uncomfortable conversation, but you need to talk openly with your parent about your anger. It may be helpful to talk with a counselor or close friend about whatever you're so angry about. You don't need to be fuming when you face your parent. Use this chance to sort out what you're really mad about.

When you talk to your parent, begin with "I love you." It's always the best way to start any talk about anger. You don't want him to think there's any doubt about your love because of this anger.

Panic   It's difficult to see your parent becoming "old," to imagine him dying. The thought of losing him can panic you—and make you feel old. As long as your parent is alive, you can still be the child. Facing your parent's mortality makes you face your own. That is hard.

Face your fears rationally. Talk to your parent about how he feels about growing older and how he felt when he lost his own parents. Aging—both his and yours—takes a little time to accept. Let it bring you together instead of keeping you apart.

27 Call a Family Meeting

Before you contradict an old man, you should endeavor to understand him.
—George Santayana

If your parent gets ill, is widowed, hits financial trouble, or becomes unable to live on his own, the problem becomes a family matter. A family meeting is a wise way to come up with the best solution. It gives everyone an opportunity to voice her opinion, takes the burden off just one or two, and prevents hasty, panicked decisions from being made during a crisis.

It might not exactly be a love-in—family emotions run high during a crisis. But in the end, your parent benefits most because you'll come up with decisions born out of honest talk instead of guilt or anger. Here's how to start.

First If possible, invite your parent. If she is too confused or ill to attend, or if the meeting would greatly upset her, then she should not be there. At the very least, let her know you're having a family conference; tell her who's coming and what you'll talk about. No secrets. This meeting is about love, caring, and respect, not about taking away all of her control over her life. Explain that the meeting could open up new options to a problem that might seem hopeless.

Second   Decide who else should be at the meeting: your own family, brothers, sisters, maybe neighbors, your parent's siblings—anyone genuinely concerned for your parent's welfare. An involved relative can bring a clearer perspective. At the meeting, state the issue or crisis at hand, and then give everyone a chance to talk. If the discussion is about your parent's increasing inability to care for herself well, start from there. Discuss her difficulties, the options, the finances, the feelings, and the fears.

Listen with love to your parent, but don't let the meeting lose its rational purpose. Her health, happiness, and safety are the important things. Work together with her as a family to make a wise decision that's best for your parent.

28 Communicate Better

The reason why we have two ears and one mouth is that we may listen the more and talk the less.
—Zeno of Citium

We've all read enough magazine articles by now to know we have to learn to communicate in our relationships. But what exactly does that mean? How do you know if you and your parent aren't really communicating? It's no easy thing. There are some common pitfalls of communication between aging parents and their kids. Here are a few do's and don'ts we've collected from counselors and seniors.

DO recognize that he may need to talk a lot about his life, to go back over his past and reassure himself that he was a good person and did his best. Gerontologists call this "Life Validation." Let him talk. Tell him, "You did well with that, Dad. I've always admired you for that."

DON'T shut her out of the problems in your life. You might be doing this to avoid bothering her, but to her it feels like rejection. Don't assume she won't understand . . . things weren't so different when she was young. Try her.

DON'T say, "Oh, Dad, you don't remember."

Maybe he doesn't. So remind him about whatever it is.

DO let her talk about death. It will be hard for you to hear her say, "I'm ready to die." Resist the urge to say, "Stop that. You're going to be fine." She needs you to listen. If you want to say something, try, "I can see how you might be feeling that way. It's hard for me because I want you to always be with me." Or "I guess we have to leave that decision to God."

DO tell her when she looks pretty, tell him when he looks handsome. Mention his blue eyes that you've loved looking into all these years; compliment the outfit she's put together.

DON'T begin a sentence with "You never . . ."

DON'T misread her body language. Older folks don't always look like they need a warm hug because aches, pains, or frailties can convey body language that's not inviting.

DO ask his opinion on the world, your world, your concerns.

DON'T speak to your parent like he's a child even though a role reversal has clearly taken place between you. It's tough on his ego and a tough adjustment for you. Talk with him about what he really needs and doesn't need, and you'll find his gratitude.

DO show that you appreciate gifts or money with a special thank-you call or, even better, a thank-you note. Have grandchildren send a thank-you note or drawing, too.

DO joke together.

DO say, "I love you." Even if you're not from the type of family that say that to each other often, you'll be surprised how fast your parent can get used to hearing you say it!

29 Understand the Retirement Blues

Work is the meat of life, pleasure the dessert.
—Bertie Charles Forbes

Ahhhh . . . retirement! The great relaxing reward for a lifetime of hard work. So why has your parent been moping around since he retired?

This is not an easy country to relax in. Everybody's rushing off to work all the time. So while individuals around him have schedules to keep, people to see, and goals to achieve, your dad suddenly feels like one of those guys who can hardly pass the day. It might have him feeling useless, bored, isolated, and old.

Projects and Hobbies You've probably had the urge to suggest all sorts of projects for him: "Why don't you finally turn your basement into a workshop?" "Study?" "Darkroom?" "Build a greenhouse?"

Or maybe you're full of ideas for hobbies he can get into. We predict you've already urged at least three of these: lawn bowling, gardening, painting, drawing, ceramics, writing, reading, photography, jogging, swimming, Bridge, cribbage, fishing, picture framing, woodworking, furniture refinishing, travel, and volunteering.

You might be dreaming of the day you have enough free time to do some of those things, but your dad might not be interested in them. Of course, you're only trying to help. But you'll find urging your parent to take on activities probably won't get you anywhere. Suggestions? Okay. But nobody wants to feel like he's being nagged. He'll find his own new interests in his own time. When he worked, he didn't have to depend on his kids for ideas on how to be productive. He could now be worrying that you see him as an elderly man. He wants you to see him as vital, not ready for the shuffleboard court.

Attitude Adjustment   Accepting retirement can be hard work. It will help if you try to understand that. In *Necessary Losses* Judith Viorst gives a tough but fair look at what retirement can do to the soul and the adjustment it takes before your parent can enjoy it. She says men have a particularly hard time letting go of the identity work gives them. Think about it. When you first meet someone, you ask his name, where he lives, and what he does for a living, right? If your parent is recently retired, he's having to ask himself, "Who am I now?"

The loss of a steady paycheck and friends at work might have him feeling isolated. And isolation makes people feel old and a little unloved. You can make a difference. You can't take on the losses for him, and you can't go through this transition for him. But you can make sure he feels loved. Affirm to him that you and your family need him very much. Spend more effort listening than talking. If he feels love, he'll find hope again. And he'll slowly begin to take control of his own sweet, and deserved, retirement.

30 Laugh Together

You don't stop laughing because you grow old. You grow old because you stop laughing.
—Michael Pritchard

Want a good laugh? Then have one! And share it with your aging parent. Go ahead and giggle, guffaw, snicker, and belly laugh together. Laughter has a magical effect on the body . . . especially on a body over 60.

A Healthy Laugh Let's take a tally of all the ways laughter can help your parent's body. We put our list together with some help from a man in Birmingham, Alabama, who has inspired many folks to crack a smile—William Travis, a retired pharmacist known for his humorous lectures on laughter and the body.

First, when he begins laughing, the muscles in his face squeeze out tears, and abdominal muscles force breath out of his lungs. It pushes out gases that have been collecting and replaces them with OXYGEN. Wastes are thrown off, like some microorganisms that cause disease. CLEARING OUT THE LUNGS this way helps to prevent pneumonia, believe it or not.

Next, laughing is really like JOGGING FOR THE HEART! At least according to Dr. William Fry who's been studying laughter for more than 30 years. He says laughter can double your parent's HEART RATE in just 20 seconds and increase the volume of blood pumped with each beat. If your parent gets very little exercise, this is the next best thing. Laugh and his heart laughs with him.

Watch your dad's face while he laughs. His SKIN enjoys the joke as much as he does . . . he'll get a rosy flush as he laughs.

ARE YOU CONVINCED YET, OR DO WE HAVE TO TICKLE YOU?

There's more. Laughing can help your parent beat the stress that comes with aging. LAUGHTER AND STRESS CAN'T EXIST TOGETHER IN THE HUMAN BODY! A good giggle helps relax the mind and provides a great weapon against the toll stress can take on his heart and blood pressure.

Speaking of blood pressure . . . some research shows that hearty laughter has improved high blood pressure in some patients. It's also helped some cases of diabetes and aids the autoimmune system in fighting off infections.

Oldest Recorded Full-Body Laugh   In Genesis 17, God told Abraham that his 90-year-old wife was going to have a baby. Abraham (age 100) laughed so hard that he rolled on the ground. Now that's a laugh!

Help Him Laugh   As his child, you are the person who has brought your parent the most smiles since the day you were born. Drag out the baby pictures and get a good giggle over what a funny-looking kid you were. Better yet, drag out your brother's and sister's baby pictures and get a good laugh at how funny looking THEY were.

Never send him a letter without a joke, cartoon, or funny family story inside. Buy him nostalgic audiotapes or videotapes from the forties and fifties.

Whatever it takes, when you visit or call, take time to laugh together. A little serious silliness will do you both good.

31 Make Room for Romance

If there is anything better than to be loved, it is loving.
—Anonymous

It's kind of funny, but most young people think love and romance are their turf exclusively. The truth is, folks over 50 have just as much claim to the mushy stuff as we do.

Tender Hearts If your parent is widowed or divorced, maybe she is happy being alone. But many single seniors would love to find a partner. It's just that their kids aren't always so comfortable with the idea of ol' mom or dad looking for love later in life. In fact, we tend to view our aging parents as sexless. We need to grow up! Snuggling, tenderness, and romance are wonderful at any age.

Most seniors give these reasons for wanting a partner:

1. Companionship
2. Security
3. Sex and romance

Those reasons aren't so different from the ones younger people give. Except maybe you were surprised to see the word *sex* in there? Consider this fact: Older people enjoy sex, too!

Two New York gerontologists recently surveyed 800 people over 60. In the 60- to 79-year-old group, 97 percent said sex was a crucial part of their lives, giving them a good feeling about themselves. For the 80- to 91-year-olds, the figure dropped down only to 93 percent saying sex was important.*

It's probably pretty awkward for both you and your parent to talk about sex. It might even be tough for him to talk to his wife or doctor about it. Still, be aware that some sexual difficulties occur as the body ages or with medications. Many problems can be easily remedied by a talk with the doctor.

Sensitive Hearts If your dad has never mentioned to you his desire to find a new love, he could be afraid of your response. Maybe you'll tell him he's silly. He may even feel a little silly himself. He might worry you'll get upset at the notion of him finding a "replacement" for your mother. If you bring it up to him in a positive way, you can make it easier for him: "Dad, you're so terrific. I'd love to see you with somebody special by your side. Do you ever think about it?" You might be surprised where the discussion goes from there!

If your parent is remarrying and you're worrying about his finances, his life-style, your role . . . the solution is the same in every case: TALK ABOUT

* Survey done by Dr. Bernard Starr from the Center for Gerontological Studies at the University of New York and Marcella Baker Weinter from Brooklyn College.

IT TOGETHER. No matter how important you are in his life, no matter how much more he depends on you these days, his emotions are his own. Open up your heart and love the one he loves, too.

32 Make a File

Knowledge is of two kinds. We know a subject ourselves, or we know where we can find information upon it.
—*Samuel Johnson*

Managing your own legal and financial affairs is tough enough; taking care of someone else's is a major undertaking. Yet eventually, you or someone in your family is going to have to manage these affairs for a parent.

Personal Records File You can make this task easier by helping your parent create a personal records file. The National Institute on Aging has compiled a list of things to put in that file.

- Full legal name; date and place of birth
- Social Security number
- Legal residence
- Names and addresses of spouse and children (or location of death certificate if any are deceased)
- Location of will or trust, birth certificate, and certificates of marriage, divorce, and citizenship
- List of employers and dates of employment
- Education and military records
- Name of church or synagogue and names of clergy

- Memberships in organizations and awards received
- Names and addresses of close friends, relatives, doctors, lawyers, and financial advisors
- Requests, preferences, or prearrangements for burial

Financial Records File   Make a second file for financial records.

- Sources of income and assets (pension funds, interest income)
- Social Security and Medicare information
- Investment income (stocks, bonds, property)
- Insurance information (life, health, property)
- Bank accounts (checking, savings, credit union)
- Location of safe deposit boxes
- Copy of most recent tax return and location of tax records for previous years
- Liabilities—what is owed to whom and when payments are due
- Mortgages and debts—how and when paid
- Credit card and charge account names and numbers
- Property taxes
- Location of personal items such as jewelry or family treasures

Note that these files don't contain important documents such as a will and stock certificates. Giving their locations is safer and also lets your parent maintain privacy.

33 Help with the Will

*We inherit nothing, truly, but what
actions make us worthy of.*
—George Chapman

Talking to your parent about his will is tough. You
want him to be with you forever. But your parent
probably wants the peace of mind of knowing special belongings, property, and money will be distributed the way he wants them to after his death,
without a lot of trouble to his family. If his will isn't
done right, that won't happen. If he asks, you can
offer practical advice.

Legal Steps   Recommend a lawyer, no matter
what. If he doesn't have one, find somebody you
trust. But before that trip to the lawyer, consider
these simple guidelines found in *The Age Care
Sourcebook* by Jean Crichton.

1. Encourage him to put the will in writing, even
though verbal wills are honored in some states.

2. Have him make a list of resources. This
means all possessions, stocks, cash, real estate,
etc. Help him round up those resources onto paper.

3. Choose an executor. Being the executor of a
will can be a big job. So big that sometimes the
executor gets a fee or percentage of the estate.
Find out if it's important to him that someone he

loves take on this job, or if he wants to specify a lawyer instead.

4. Find witnesses. Witnesses shouldn't be people who are named in the will. The number of witnesses needed when a will is signed varies from state to state. The lawyer can answer this.

5. Help him choose a place to keep the will. The lawyer can keep a copy of the will. But your parent probably wants to keep his own copy. Somebody in the family needs to be told where that copy will be. Remember, safe deposit boxes aren't great places for this. In some states those boxes are sealed after the renter dies.

6. Remind him to review it. Life changes so fast. New grandchildren may come, or your parent might move to a different state. He might suddenly discover he actually is the original owner of the Brooklyn Bridge! Wouldn't want that going to just anybody. He needs to review his will periodically.

Helping your parent prepare a will is a labor of love you'd probably like to avoid. It's difficult. But it's important. While you're at it, what a time this would be to let him know the one asset he's already given you is his lifetime of love . . . and you'll carry *that* in your heart forever.

34 The Nursing Home: Find Your Role

'Tis late when an old man comes to know he is old.
—Thomas Fuller

The day your parent moves into an elder-care home may be the first day he really feels "old"—or it may just be the first day *you* see him that way. No matter how much he needs the care he can get in a home, this day can be even more traumatic for you than for him. Many older people are ready to face this phase. If he's been in the hospital, he may be ready to move on to a home. If he's been in your home, he may be relieved to stop worrying that he's been in the way. If he's been living alone, he may be looking forward to being around other people his age again.

Whatever the case, here are some guidelines to help you demonstrate how much you care.

Get Personal Different homes have different rules about which personal items residents can bring with them. But his room, or half of the room, needs his personal touch. Ask if your parent can bring along his favorite chair or reading lamp. If not, you can still encourage him to bring family pictures, plants, knickknacks, books, a bedspread, potpourri, music box, whatever. He needs his own things around him to feel safe and in some control.

Visit Frequently, But . . .   Experts tell us you shouldn't plan to visit constantly right at the beginning. You will want to. You will worry that you need to be there. But your parent needs to cope with this change himself. You will be anxious to handle everything for him, but you can't. Put your guilt away as best you can. Let him know you are thinking of him and love him.

When you do visit, come with things to talk about and be open to listen. Go for a walk together. Just *do your best.* Listen to him when he needs to be listened to. Be part of his life, and let him continue to be part of yours.

Enter and Sign In, Please   Your parent might get grouchy sometimes and complain that nobody ever comes to see him. It could be that he forgets the visits quickly. Give him a guestbook. Let the kids draw smiley faces in there; have adults leave warm messages. You can show the book to him and read the messages. Show it off to his friends and the staff at the nursing home so he can beam with pride at how loved he is to have all these great visitors.

"The Food Here Is Terrible"   Chances are good your parent will complain about the food. If he is on a special diet, he will most certainly complain about the food. You may want to try some of

the food and talk to the dietician preparing the menus. But keep in mind that people *always* complain about institutional food—when they go off to college, to camp, to the army. It is difficult to prepare healthy food for large numbers of people, ask them to eat at the same place every day, and not hear complaints. Most homes do their best to vary the meals and keep the residents healthy and reasonably happy with the food. You can ask the staff to help you make sure he is eating enough, and if his diet permits, you can take him out periodically for a special dinner to make him happier.

Get Staff Savvy   Be friendly to the staff. Spend time talking to them, especially the head of nursing. The better you know the people who care for your parent every day, the more you'll hear about what's happening in your parent's life. These are busy people, but a little warmth on your part can go a long way. You have the right to get involved, and most staffers will appreciate your good intentions. People who work in nursing homes aren't doing it to get rich! They choose this difficult work out of caring. If they realize you appreciate their efforts, those good feelings cannot help but be transferred to the way they look after your parent.

Note: If you ever have a serious concern about a staffer's performance, talk to the staff person and her superior. Move up the administrative chain until you get the answers you want. If you don't get a good response, you can lodge a complaint with the state Department of Health or move your parent to a better home.

Phone Home   If you don't live near your parent, make a plan for calling him regularly. He may not like phones. He may not do well on the phone. But try it at first. Write often, and talk to the staff about reading the letters and cards to him if he can't see well. Send along pictures, drawings, funny sayings, interesting newspaper clippings . . . anything at all when you send off the letter. Talk with the head of nursing periodically about your parent, even if you have never met her.

Find a Friend   If you live far away, find a friend or relative living near your parent's nursing home who will go by there now and then to say hello.

The Doctor   You should know how to reach your parent's doctor at any time, even if you are far away. Let your parent know you can reach the doctor if he needs you to. It will give him peace of mind.

35 Face Forgetfulness

I finally got it together. But I forgot where I put it.
—Anonymous

When someone over 55 forgets things, he feels old, frustrated, and out of control. Most of all, he might be fearful that his memory losses are a sign of mental decline. That is largely a myth, and he needs to know that.

Mental Workout Some memory problems are natural with aging. But your parent doesn't have to fully accept them. Memory lapses are just something he has to find a strategy for. His mind is a muscle that needs a regular workout to function at its best. You can help him work that muscle . . . and probably even help your own memory along the way.

Your first job is to convince your dad that his memory problems aren't a sign of something more serious. He may fear he has Alzheimer's. Very, very few forgetful people turn out to have Alzheimer's. He should talk to his doctor if he's really concerned.

Some drugs can affect the memory. If your parent is on any medication, check with the doctor or pharmacist to see if that could be the case.

Some common factors make memory problems worse in later years. Your parent might be . . .

- reading less.
- hearing poorly.
- seeing poorly.
- testing his knowledge less.
- distracted by other problems in his life
- believing he's losing his memory—and creating a self-fulfilling prophecy.

Reassure him that his lapses are not something to be upset over. If he can stop stressing out over his forgetfulness, he can work out the memory muscles.

At the Jewish Community Center in Atlanta, counselor Phyllis Shavin holds classes to help seniors exercise their memories with everyday activities: crossword puzzles, card games, word games, and a daily check of the newspaper help keep the brain "muscle" in shape. Try these ideas with your parent.

If he spends a lot of time alone, the TV may be numbing his memory. Encourage him to pay attention to how much of his time he spends in front of the "box." Instead of talking about TV shows, talk to him about the decisions he made that day, the people he met, the smells, the sounds, the things he felt, something that made him laugh—all to help him get in the habit of noticing, recalling, remembering.

Solutions Here are solutions to specific memory problems experienced by older people.

PROBLEM: Constantly misplaced keys, glasses, and dentures.

SOLUTION: Help form a habit of placing each in the same place all the time: keys near the door, eyeglasses on the night table, dentures in a special cup in the bathroom.

PROBLEM: Forgetting medication.

SOLUTION: The best solution is to buy a seven-day plastic pill holder. It's easy to carry around, and you can find one with divisions specially made for folks who need to take pills several times every day. Have your parent fill up his pill holder every Sunday night.

PROBLEM: Confusion over whether or not he paid bills.

SOLUTION: First, he can keep all bills in one place, folder, or clip. Then, he needs to get into the habit of writing the amount of each check in the register before writing the check. Or maybe he would like a checkbook with a carbon instead of a check register.

PROBLEM: Forgetting what to buy, forgetting errands.

SOLUTIONS: Lists, lists, lists! Make sure he has a pad of paper and pen in a central place in the house or his room. Throughout the week he can get in the habit of always writing down every item he runs out of, every errand that comes to mind.

And while we're on the subject of forgetfulness, let's try to remember one thing: *Nobody's memory is perfect.* Reassure your parent that his doesn't have to be. If you can help him develop just a little more skill and confidence in his memory, he'll feel younger and more in control.

36 Inspire Exercise

My grandmother started walking 5 miles a day when she was 60. She's 97 now, and we don't know where the heck she is.
—Comedienne Ellen DeGeneris

Want to know the most incredible, undeniable, amazing way to change your parent's life for the better? Inspire her to try a little exercise. Really.

Even if your parent has never exercised, is disabled in some way, or is over 75, the right level of exercise can be like a miracle. How about some of these benefits?

She will

- sleep better.
- build stronger bones and stop osteoporosis in progress.
- be able to get out of a chair easier.
- work her heart and help ward off or recover from heart trouble.
- gain strength and stamina for gardening, hobbies, and housework.
- keep her weight down.
- find self-confidence and independence!

Amazing is right! Your parent's doctor should be consulted before any exercise program is started. But if you're worried the doctor will nix the idea, don't. The couch potato life-style isn't any healthier for older folks than it is for us.

Here are some simple suggestions for starting an exercise program for an aging parent, time-tested by exercise physiologist Dee Massengale.

The Big W   Walking! For starters, have her walk twice a day for 5 minutes. It doesn't matter how fast she can walk. If she normally uses a cane or walker, she can still join the walking brigade! If you live near her and can go along, wonderful.

Increase the walk to 7 minutes, then 9 minutes the next week, then 11 minutes, then 13, and so on. Again, speed doesn't matter.

If you can help her organize a group to walk with every other day, walking can become even more of a fun routine.

Note on walking: It's effective in the fight against osteoporosis. Walking won't reverse it, but it can halt it.

Strrrrrrretch   Stretching is important for your older parent to do before walking. For folks who can't walk or who have arthritis, it's good exercise all by itself for increasing flexibility and range of motion. Remember every stretch should be held until the count of 20 to work. For 3 good stretches she should do the following:

1. Lie down on her back. Gently pull her left leg up as close to her chest as possible, hold, return to the floor. Do the same with the right leg. Repeat several times.

2. Gently roll her head to the left, hold, front, hold, right, hold. No one should ever roll the head back.

3. Stand or sit and reach one arm up to the sky, and hold. Then the other. Repeat several times.

She should NEVER risk back injury by doing anything that looks like "the twist" or bend over and touch her toes.

To avoid cramps during any type of exercise, your parent should avoid fatty foods starting 2 hours before exercise. That means no cheese, chocolate, or peanut butter. A little juice just before a walk or stretch is okay.

Arm Aerobics   Even if she's confined to a bed or wheelchair, she can still get some exercise. Just moving her arms around gets the blood pumping through her heart and works that heart muscle. Arm aerobics also build upper-body strength.

Folks who are in bed or a chair can begin twice a week for 5 minutes and increase from there. Arm aerobics are as simple as turning on a little music and adding movements like these:

- Punch up to the ceiling.
- Punch out in front.
- Hold hands up at face level and clap to music.
- Gently tap hands on top of head to the music.

The more that exercise becomes a part of your parent's life, the younger, stronger, more useful, and self-confident you'll see her become. It's not the fountain of youth . . . but so far it's the closest thing to it.

37 Medication: Ask All About It!

Take two of these and call me in the morning.
—Marcus Welby, M.D.

Have you noticed those doctors on TV? Whether it's Marcus Welby or the guys on "General Hospital," they all smile at their patients, hand them a prescription, and send them on their merry TV ways. Have you ever seen a patient on TV say, "Doc, before we go to a commercial, can you tell me what interactions could be involved with this? Side effects? Does it come in a liquid form because I really can't swallow pills very well anymore? And since I can't read your handwriting, can we go over just when and how I'm supposed to take this?"

On TV shows there isn't time for that kind of talk! But in real life you and your parent have to make time in that office and at the pharmacist's counter to ask questions about any prescription.

Top Three Reasons People Don't Ask Their Doctor Questions:

1. "He's so busy."
2. "I don't want to offend her."
3. "I'm sure the doctor tells me everything I need to know."

Do any of these reasons sound familiar? They're

all understandable. Doctor's offices are intimidating places!

Doctor Visits   Plan to go with her to the doctor. Even if your parent is able to drive herself, speak for herself, and understand for herself, ask her if you can go and take the notes. And it might be easier for your mom if you ask the questions. Grab your pencil, paper, and this list for starters.
Ask the doctor:

- "Do you feel like we've given you a clear picture of her symptoms and concerns today?"
- "Are there any side effects to the drug you're prescribing? If so, which ones indicate that we should call you?"
- "When should this drug be taken? How often? With food? Without? What foods could interfere?"
- "May we have the written information that comes with this drug?"
- "Here's a written list of the other drugs my mom is taking, including nonprescription drugs she takes regularly or occasionally. Did I leave anything off that you know of? Do you see any interaction problems?"
- "My mom is seeing a specialist who has prescribed something for her. Are you aware of that, and could the drug you're prescribing be the same thing only under a different name due to different manufacturers?"

- "She prefers (capsules, liquid, pills)—could the drug come in this form for her?"
- "How should this be stored? In the fridge?"

Unfortunately, doctors are among the most famous interrupters and impatient listeners you'll find. If you don't get every question answered, talk to your pharmacist. It's not a bad idea to find a pharmacist you and your mom feel comfortable with and stick with him. If you live in another city from your parent, call and ask these questions over the phone. If you feel like the doctor is annoyed with this scavenger hunt for information, you and your mom might want to go on a hunt for a new doctor. A good doctor will be thrilled to have you on his team.

Books   Take a trip to the bookstore and buy *The Pill Book* (Bantam).

The more you know, the better you'll both feel. With you by her side, your parent has a great advantage in staying safe and healthy in the prescription drug maze.

38 Rotate the Occasions

And young and old come forth to play
on a sunshine holiday.
—John Milton

In most families of grown children, one sibling usually ends up being the social chairperson: planning the holidays, organizing parents' anniversary party, asking everyone to pitch in for a special Mother's Day gift—and getting stuck with the bill when the black sheep of the family doesn't pay up.

Party Planning If you're the unelected social director of your family, here's something you can do to lighten the load. At the next family gathering, corner your siblings and divide the occasions among you. For example, if there are 5 of you, you might do it this way:

Eldest:	Mother's Day
#2:	Father's Day
#3:	Mom's Birthday
#4:	Dad's Birthday
Youngest:	Their Anniversary

If your family is smaller, you'll have to take more than one (and if you're an only child, no wonder you're the chairperson).

Each person makes sure that that day is special for your parents, whether it means organizing a party or setting up a gift pool.

39 Valentine's Day

Who loves ya, baby?
—Kojak

Valentine's Day isn't just a day for lovers—it's a chance for everybody to celebrate love. Don't leave your parent out of the celebration on February 14.

There are lots of ways to say, "I love you." Here's an even dozen for you to show your parent she's a special valentine.

Embroider I LOVE YOU on a pillowcase. It only takes 23 big stitches.

Donate blood to the Red Cross, or give money to the Heart Association in her name.

Dedicate a song to her on that favorite oldies station she loves.

Tie a red ribbon around her dog's or cat's collar.

Discover her needs by giving her 5 index cards with a heart drawn up in the corner. Ask her to write down a task or favor on each card and give them back to you. Promise that you'll finish them all by St. Patty's Day.

Play a game of Hearts together. If she lives in a nursing or retirement home, invite some of her friends to join in.

Serve a spot of tea and some heart cookies for an afternoon Valentine's Day tea together. Again, invite her friends.

Send her a big red paper heart and write "I love you" on it in as many languages as you can find. Here's help: "Je t'aime" (French); "Ich liebe dich" (German); "Ti amo" (Italian); "Te amo" (Spanish); "Jag alskar dig" (Swedish); "I love you" (English!).

Draw a big red heart on her mirror in red lipstick. (And remember to come back the next day with the window cleaner.)

Celebrate the years if your parents are together. Send them a box of red-hots and a note that says, "To the Last of the Red-Hot Lovers."

Hold a St. Valentine's Day Stickup. Stick hearts all over everything. If she's in the hospital, put heart stickers from the nurse's cap to the bedpan. If she's far away, send a valentine with the envelope covered in hearts . . . and enclose her own sheet of heart stickers to stick up herself.

It doesn't have to be a big deal . . . just remember your parent on Valentine's Day. It'll do your own heart good, too.

40 Passover

Do not remove the ancient landmark which your fathers have set.
—*Proverbs 22:28*

Both Christians and Jews can celebrate Passover. It's a celebration of the exodus of the Israelites from Egypt. A glorious, tradition-filled family feast!

Seder The Exodus story is a powerful one. Make a commitment as a family to each read your parts of it with the drama and passion it was written with so long ago.

Special Teacher These days many families invite friends to Seder who aren't Jewish. With so many mixed marriages there may be grandchildren who don't know much about Passover. Give your parent the role of explaining the food and traditions to your guests and the children. They should know they're eating matzo because unleavened bread symbolizes the way the exiles lived. Let her explain to your Christian guests that the Last Supper was a Seder. Most people feel closer to their faith as they get older. On this family holiday when elders are so important, she will enjoy the role of teacher.

Private Time   Passover can be a busy time
with so much family all around. Don't let the holiday fly by without a little time alone with your parent. How about a just-the-two-of-you popcorn party
before Passover? You can even make it a new private tradition. Once your hearts are filled and the
popcorn bowl is empty, share the tradition of
cleaning the house of all the unleavened bread.

41 Thanksgiving

We gather together to ask the Lord's blessing.
—Thanksgiving song

What a blessing it is to have several generations of your glorious family gathered together. Thanksgiving is a day for you and your parent to do exactly what the Pilgrims and Indians did—give thanks that your brave little band has weathered another year of storms, planted, nurtured, and harvested . . . and now come together again to celebrate your blessings.

The Food If your family feast is one where everybody makes some contribution to the event . . . LET YOUR PARENT BE PART OF THAT PROCESS, TOO. She doesn't want to be left out! Let her bring her world-famous yam recipe even if she rarely cooks. If she is unable to cook, ask her to send you the recipe in advance so she can still contribute to the menu.

The Blessing Talk to your parent in advance about giving the blessing at the beginning of the meal. He may want to prepare something special. Even if your family has never been the type to hold hands and listen to a Thanksgiving blessing, try it this year. You can even go around the table and each tell something special that happened this year that you're thankful for. Your parent will beam with pride . . . and you can all fill up your hearts feeling great before you start filling up your stomachs with turkey.

The Children If you have a kid's table at your Thanksgiving feast, offer your parent the chance to sit with the little ones instead of the grown-ups this year. You might be surprised if he thinks it would be a hoot! We know one family patriarch who groans every year if he doesn't get to sit with the kids. He says they talk about the most fun stuff . . . and let him have the extra rolls.

Welcome Thanksgiving is the busiest time of year at airports. But wouldn't your parent love to see as many of you as possible welcoming him when he steps off that plane? Make a point to round up as many family folks as possible . . . and everybody greet him with "Welcome Grandpa" signs. If he lives in town but you've got other relatives flying in, invite your dad to make the airport trip with you. If going to the airport is just too much for your parent, make his place the first stop on the way home from the airport for a welcome party that comes to him.

Special Time Of course you'll want some time alone with your parent on this holiday, but that can be tough. You can steal some time around the kitchen table while the rest of the gang huddle

around the football games. Or share a blanket together on the sidelines if there's a game of touch
football going in the backyard. If you're both early
risers, make an early date for Thanksgiving breakfast together on Turkey Day. Or conspire to sneak
into the kitchen that night, and take off with left-
over turkey sandwiches on a drive together.

Thankfulness Finally . . . let your parent
know somehow that you're thankful to have him in
your life. If it's hard to say face-to-face, leave him a
note on the mirror, or put a card in her suitcase
she'll find when she gets home from the holiday.

42 Christmas

The only gift is a portion of thyself.
—Emerson

Here is our stocking full of suggestions for how to make this Christmas special for your aging parent.

Give him his own Christmas star. Call the International Star Registry at 1-800-282-3333. For under $40, a real star will be named for him, registered in that name, and copyrighted at the Library of Congress. They'll also give your parent a "map of the heavens" to show where his star is and an official certificate proving he is, in fact, totally heavenly.

Holiday Hams   If your parent can be with the family for Christmas, put on a supersimple family Christmas pageant for her. Just let family members know a month in advance that they should bring their favorite Christmas memory, poem, song, Bible passage—whatever! Then you can sit down together around her (and a big stack of cookies, of course) and share your Christmas selections. Invite her to share her favorite, too.

Christmas Dinner   If she's coming for Christmas dinner, call in advance to ask if there's anything special she'd like to eat or any foods she's been having trouble with lately. Also ask if she has a favorite recipe she'd like to make or share with you so you can make it.

Church Hop   Go to *her* church instead of yours.

Kiss Noel   Seal his day with a Christmas kiss. Give him mistletoe for his lapel or cap, and make sure everybody plants a big one on his cheek.

Safe Holiday   If your parent visits only during holidays, do a safety check before he comes. Set night-lights leading to the bathroom; apply no-slip fixtures to the bottom of the tub; remove throw rugs he could trip over.

Talk and Touch   Find time alone with your parent amidst the Christmas chaos to talk and to share an unhurried holiday hug.

Holiday I Love You's   This is a holiday of love—let him know that by saying, "I love you." Sing it, sew it, shout it from the front yard at the stroke of midnight . . . just say it. If you find it just too hard to say, write I LOVE YOU in gold glitter on a giant card he can put in his room.

Simple Christmas   If she lives in a home, take a little Christmas to her room with some decorations. Keep it simple, nothing that will get in her way.

Family of Friends   Ask her if she has any friends she would like to bring over for a holiday meal. Or take the celebration to her nursing home and make an effort to invite some of her friends to join you.

Memorial Drive   Christmas is a time of memories. If your parent has lost someone close to him, offer to drive him to the cemetery at some point during the holidays to visit the grave.

Unpack for the Holidays   When she's packing to go home, sneak a treat into her suitcase. The post–holiday blues won't hit so hard if she unpacks her stuff and finds a picture from Christmas morning, a homemade "coupon" for a New Year's Day lunch or long-distance call, or just a thank-you note for a wonderful visit.

43 Birthdays

*How old would you be if you didn't
know how old you was?*
—*Satchel Paige*

There's nothing more boring than people who
don't like to celebrate birthdays. The fact is, a
birthday isn't really about becoming a year older.
It's simply a wonderful excuse to give someone an
annual gift of a day all her own! Nobody is too old
to feel special. No matter how your parent feels
about growing older, let her know you think she's
something to celebrate.

Sing Forget sitting around the table singing
"Happy Birthday" so slowly it sounds like a record
played at the wrong speed. Do your best Bing
Crosby imitation, perform it to the tune of "Camp-
town Races," give it a Jamaican beat, get the whole
family to rehearse a little harmony, get that sax out
of the attic and horn in on the song—anything to
give this performance a new touch.

Long-Distance Touch. Record this musical masterpiece on audiotape or videotape, and send it off so
she can play it on her big day. Or call long distance
and perform it live.

More than Cake Cake does not a birthday make. Here are some alternatives to serving the usual cake and ice cream from Wicke Chambers and Spring Asher in their book *Celebrations*. Prepare a wheel of brie with a circle of apples around it and "Happy Birthday" in squirt cheese on top of the brie. Serve up a bowl of punch but with a twinkle; float candles in lemon slices. Write "Happy Birthday" on a pizza with green peppers. Birthday Breakfast Quiche . . . with bacon bits in a heart shape on top.

Long-Distance Touch. Cakes don't mail well, but brownies and giant chocolate chip cookies do. Or call a bakery in your parent's neighborhood and ask if they can deliver a cake and charge it to your credit card.

Kids Let the little ones in the family read a birthday story to your mom or dad. Dr. Seuss wrote a book called *Happy Birthday to You!* Wrap it up for your parent and let the kids treat her to an on-the-spot reading.

Beyond Greeting Cards Before you mail off a card, grab a couple of family members and go to K-Mart. Buy some of those funny hats and noise-makers. Then head to the photobooth and throw an instant party for the camera! For a couple of bucks, you'll have 4 pictures in about 2 minutes. Slide the pictures inside the card for the silliest birthday smiles she's ever seen.

Birthday Lunch   Invite some of her friends to birthday lunch. Even if she lives in a nursing home, make a formal invitation to some of her friends to join you for lunch in the cafeteria or just for cake in her room.

Put your own loving style into your parent's birthday and it will just naturally become a day to remember. What you're really celebrating is her.

44

Weddings

To have and to hold, from this day forward.
—The Book of Common Prayer

Weddings are love rituals. They bring together traditions, families, cultures, religions, and memories. A wedding day is particularly special to an older family member because so many of her descendants are gathered together to celebrate. So where do your parents, the grandparents of the bride and groom, fit in? Or maybe you're getting married a little later in life and you're not sure how to include your own aging parents? Here are some ideas.

Announcements Let your wedding guests know that you have the honor of having grandparents with you to celebrate. Ask the minister or rabbi to mention during his remarks the privilege of having them there. Introduce them at an appropriate time at the reception.

Involvement If possible, let grandparents take a role in the celebration. Bea and Thore Johnson are in their eighties but spirited and more than healthy enough to make the long trip to their grandsons' weddings. Guests raised their glasses as they listened to Thore give the first toast of the celebration. His speech was short . . . and he and

his bride of more than 60 years smiled, sipped together, and toasted their growing family. What better affirmation can a new marriage have?

Memories   Around the cake table, place pictures from weddings past, including your parents'
and grandparents' wedding portraits right in front.
Also, ask your mom if she has a pretty family table-
cloth to drape the cake table.

Tradition   Parents and grandparents wear cor-
sages and boutonnieres. For a special touch, find
out what type of flower they wore at their own weddings, and have the florist include it. Nostalgia always smells sweet.

Hand-Me-Downs   Suggest to your parent that
the best wedding gift he can give isn't in the registry . . . it's in his attic.

Quick Pictures   Pictures from professional
photographers are great, but they can take forever
to arrive and are costly. Grandparents usually get
one, maybe two pictures from the wedding, and
they arrive six months or a year after the big day.
Here's a better idea: In addition to the fancy professional pictures, bring your own camera to the wedding, and snap your own memories at the reception.

When you drop off the film, ask for a couple of
extra sets of prints. Grandparents would love to

find an envelope full of pictures arrive along with a thank-you note for being on hand for the big day.

Special note: Make the effort to gather up every family member there for one group picture. There are so few chances to snap this moment, and the grandparents of the newlyweds will cherish this.

Chairpeople Receiving lines can be tedious and difficult for older folks who aren't used to standing for long periods. But of course your guests should meet the family patriarch and matriarch. Ask them if they'd rather sit with the guestbook . . . that way they can chat briefly with everyone who arrives. This is also perfect for parents in wheelchairs.

45 Memorial Days

We must always have old memories, and young hopes.
—Arsène Houssaye

Widows say that one of the toughest things about a spouse's death is the loss of someone to reminisce with. They shared decades of moments together and recorded most of them not on film or videotape, but in the memory. Now that the spouse is gone, there's no one who can fully appreciate the replaying of these memories. Except you.

Replay some of these memories with her. By doing so you'll give her a healthy opportunity to reminisce and affirm the importance of the person who meant the most to her.

The memory goes into serious rewind on "memorial days"—significant dates such as their anniversary, his birthday, and the anniversary of his death. These are the days you *know* she's thinking about him. You can make these memorial days special by acknowledging that you are, too.

A Birthday Call   A birthday is a time to celebrate the fact that the person entered the world—and your life has been enriched because of it. (And in the case of a parent—you *exist* because of it!) If your dad were alive today, you'd be calling to wish him "Happy Birthday." So why not call your mom to tell her you're happy he was born? Tell her some of the priceless things he taught you and how he enriched the lives of others. Ask her to tell you some of these things, too.

A Letter Your parents' partnership changed the world in small and not-so-small ways. Remind her of the effect they've had on family and friends and community. Tell her what you miss now that he's gone.

A Visit Reminisce together. Ask her to describe some of her favorite memories. For example, if it's their wedding anniversary, have her tell you (again) all about their courtship, engagement, and wedding.

46 Dementia: Coping with Confusion

There is no fear in love.
—Jesus

If your parent is often confused, it may frighten you, upset you, and leave you feeling helpless. You may find visiting her extremely difficult—you might even have been avoiding it. Those feelings are all completely normal. But even if she doesn't recognize who you are, *don't think your visits are a waste of time!* They absolutely are not.

Be There If she doesn't know who you are, who your children are, or exactly where she is . . . be there for her. Sit with her. Hold her hand. Watch TV with her. If she's nonresponsive, bring your reading and sit in the chair near her. Knit. Grade papers. What's important is that you're there. Many health workers we talked to believe that, despite the blank stares, there are still emotions inside. Believe that your being there brings love to her life. You make a difference.

Karin Green's grandmother came to live in the nursing home where Karin ran the physical therapy department. Grams was in her nineties and didn't remember Karin anymore. People would remind Grams that this was her granddaughter, yet she could not make that connection in her mind.

But over time Karin took on the role of Grams's "special person." She knew that Karin was someone who cared about her and came by to see her every day, hold her hand, and ask about her day. Grams was very lucky. Of course you can't be there every day. Just do the best you can. Your parent needs her own "special person." Let it be you.

Give Love   It might upset you to hear your parent speak nonsensically. You may have the urge to quiz her, thinking that somehow, this will bring her back to reality: "What day is this?" "Who is president?" "Can you count backward from 100?" The doctor may do this. But *you* don't need to put your parent to a test. Does it really matter if she knows today is Thursday? In our world, yes. In her world, no. *Don't try to make your parent talk sense.* If she has lost her connection to our world, what she needs from you is your touch, your voice, and your caring.

This is a tough act of love on your part because you may not see much response from her. But feeling love will help take away her fears. Giving love will help take away yours.

47 Depression: Living with Loss

Enthusiasm in maturity—that's the great trick of life.
—Dr. Fred Plum

Being cheerful and full of hope is hard enough when you're young. It takes some real effort when a person is feeling the effects of aging. Your parent is facing feelings you can't really understand yet . . . feelings that can bring depression. The later years bring many losses, big and small. They all take some mourning. It will help your parent if you are sensitive to some of her "low" times.

Here are some of the most common feelings of loss and causes of depression in older folks. Atlanta gerontological counselor Phyllis Shavin says her seniors struggle with these losses often.

Loss of Health Even the healthiest senior deals with some physical reminders of aging: aches, pains, eye and ear problems, stomach troubles, etc., etc., etc. Gerontologists give this recipe for any young person who wants a taste of aging in an instant: Put cotton in your ears and pebbles in your shoes. Put on a pair of rubber gloves. Then smear petroleum jelly all over the lenses of your glasses. Try an hour of that and see how it feels. It can be frustrating.

The fact is, losing even the tiniest bits of good

health is a loss. She's realizing that she may never feel 100 percent healthy again.

Your parent may be mourning the loss of her health. Even if you can't fix her aches and pains, listening to her frustrations with them will help.

Loss of Loved Ones Think about how many of your parent's friends and relatives have passed away in the last few years. It's very hard to lose so many important people and hard for your parent not to think about her own death. Let her mourn.

Loss of Control If she can't drive, set her own meal schedule, look after her own health problems . . . whatever . . . your parent is losing the control she once had over her life. That is no small thing. No matter how old a person is, feeling like she can't control her own daily life is a major part of depression. Make sure she has at least a few things in her life that she CAN control.

Let her make up her own shopping list, collect her own coupons, choose her own hairstyle, fold her sweaters the way she likes them folded, wear gloves in August, or ride in the backseat even though there's nobody in the passenger seat up front if it makes her happier. Ask her before you come to visit; always knock on her door before you come in.

You may find your parent needs to talk to folks her own age to really deal with the depression that comes with the losses of aging. "The mere process of growing old together will make our slightest acquaintances seem like bosom-friends," according to Logan Pearsall Smith. Encourage her to seek out a group for cards, arts and crafts . . . any situation that would find her some kindred spirits.

If she's in a nursing home, talk with the counselor or activities director there about encouraging your parent to get into some sort of group situation. Or talk to the counselor at her local community or senior citizens center.

48 Alzheimer's: Easing the Journey

The butterfly counts not months, but moments.
—Rabin-Dranath Tagore

Caring for a parent with Alzheimer's can break your heart. That's why they call it "the long good-bye." But instead of seeing this good-bye as an end, you can see it as a journey you can ease for him.

You and your mom or dad have said good-bye many times over the years. Smiles, tears, touches, hugs. The years with Alzheimer's can bring all those things for you both. You're facing tremendous responsibility. But it's your chance to make this the most caring and loving good-bye of a lifetime.

The Stages You need to understand that Alzheimer's is a disease that seems to go through stages. It's hard to predict how fast your parent will progress through them. The course of Alzheimer's usually takes from 3 to 15 years. A basic guideline is that the later in life he gets the disease, the slower it progresses. It's a "long good-bye" indeed. But practical suggestions can help you ease the journey once your parent is tentatively diagnosed with Alzheimer's.

Frustration Fixers Save your parent some of the frustration that comes with memory loss with some simple ideas for a house or even her room if she lives in a home.

- Avoid moving things around. Seeing the chair, jewelry box, or mirror in the same place every day is a memory helper and could be part of her method for sticking to a routine.
- Label important doors around the house, either with a word like *garage* or with a colorful picture of a car, for example. You can do the same thing for her drawers. Put a photograph of each person on his or her bedroom door (and even on her own room or over her bed if she's in a nursing home).
- Label hot and cold faucets. Make hot in red, cold in black.
- Make a gigantic calendar for the wall. Let kids or grandkids decorate it or even draw it.
- Buy a few large digital clocks. Give her a digital watch.

Face-to-Face Talking and listening can be hard for both of you.

- Don't walk around the room when you're talking to your parent. Face him. Look into his eyes. Lower your voice a little to a soft, low pitch. Speak slowly.

- Ask questions one at a time. Don't say, "Would you like to have lunch with me at Bob's? Do you still have that green tie? That would look great. Do you know which tie I mean?" First ask him to lunch. After you get an answer, ask about the tie.

- It'll often be hard for your parent to communicate what he wants. Allow for long silences while he thinks. Help by asking simple step-by-step yes or no questions to decode what he's trying to say. If you suspect he is having some pain or discomfort, try pointing to different places on his body and let him nod yes or no. If he constantly repeats the same word or sentence or has extreme difficulty, say, "It's okay," so he knows you are not frustrated by his problem.

- Touch. It's always easier to listen or talk if someone you love is holding your hand!

- Laugh, smile, play, sing together. Even the tiniest actions of joy will touch you both.

Take Care of Yourself When things get tough, lean on the folks at the Alzheimer's Association. Their motto is "Someone to stand by me," and they'll be there for you and your parent with information and perspective. They have support groups that meet in homes, churches, nursing homes, and hospitals. This is a place to talk about guilt, frustration, fear, anger—emotions that can be hard to admit in front of friends who aren't close to an Alzheimer's patient. If your head is clear and your face is smiling, the days will be brighter for your parent!

49 Be Safe

An ounce of prevention is worth a pound of cure.
—Ben Franklin

Whether your parent lives alone or with you, visits you, or lives in a nursing home, you need to be smart about safety. Take action.

Bathroom

- Lock away all electrical appliances like hair dryers and razors. They could end up in the tub.
- Turn down the temperature on your hot water heater. She may have trouble judging how hot the water is getting.
- Lock up all medicines.
- Install grab bars around the tub and toilet.
- Put no-slip strips in tub.

Hallways and Stairways

- Put night-lights in hallways, especially on the route from bedroom to bath.
- Avoid throw rugs.
- Make sure railings are secure.
- Keep steps clear of all clutter.

- Sometimes it's hard to see the edge of each step. Mark each one with bright tape.
- Block bottom and top of stairwell if necessary.

Kitchen

- Unplug appliances like blenders or mixers.
- Lock up knives.
- Keep on the lookout for cracks in dishes or glasses.
- Have a fire extinguisher on hand for all types of fires. Also install smoke alarms here and throughout the house.
- Plug up unused electrical outlets here and around the house with plastic plugs available at the hardware store.

There are other ways to help avoid falls. Keep phone and electrical cords tucked out of the way. Don't use too much wax on floors. Make sure hems of pants, skirts, and sleeves aren't too long so they get in her way. Check the soles of her shoes and slippers. If they're too worn, they're dangerous. Make sure things she needs regularly, such as eyeglasses, tissues, and coffee mug, are easily reachable so she won't fall trying to get them.

50 Arthritis: Getting a Grip

Happiness isn't a destination but a way of traveling.
It's how you manage your whole life that counts.
—Guide to Independent Living for People with Arthritis

Arthritis is debilitating at worst, aggravating at best. If your parent has arthritis, you've seen how the daily pain of normal tasks can bring him down.

Doctors still don't know what causes arthritis or how to cure it. All they can do is treat it. What you can do as the child of a parent with arthritis is to help him learn to manage his daily life, which will eliminate some of the pain. The less pain he has, the happier and more independently he can live.

You need some clever thinking and some gadgets. Then you can set up his house or room to make normal tasks easier for him. The great news is that the Arthritis Foundation puts out an awesome book full of ideas and suggestions called *Guide to Independent Living for People with Arthritis*. (It's very inexpensive, and we'll tell you how to get it at the end of this chapter.)

For Easier Eating Give him . . .

- plates with a lip around the outer edge to make it easier to get food off the plate.

- a thin disk of rubber or nonskid surface pad to put under the plate to keep it from sliding.
- a pizza cutter to cut food with a simple rolling motion rather than a knife.
- rubber bicycle grips to slip over utensil handles for easier grabbing.

For Working around the House
Give . . .

- kitchen or workman's aprons with full pockets. He can keep small items in the pockets and make fewer trips, even carry enough silverware to set the table without going back and forth to the kitchen.
- a rolling utility cart to move heavier things around the house.
- long-handled dustpan, brush, and tub scrubber to avoid bending down to clean.
- a lightweight sweeper to take the place of light vacuuming. If there's no one else who can handle the heavier vacuuming, give him a lightweight electric broom instead of a heavy vacuum.
- a pizza paddle for tucking in sheets and blankets under the mattress to make the bed.
- a laundry cart on wheels.
- a lightweight iron with automatic shutoff or a clothes steamer to eliminate ironing entirely.
- a fuzzy machine washable mitt for dusting without bending fingers.

- long metal tongs for reaching things and for turning food in the oven.

For the Bathroom   Give . . .

- a plastic dental floss holder.
- toothpaste in a pump instead of a tube.
- a cordless electric razor.
- a round "Flicker" razor for ladies for an easier grip.

For Clothes   Give . . .

- shirts and bottoms with large flat buttons or sew Velcro tabs behind each button.
- tassles, rings, or loops that can be added to a zipper pull for easier grasping.
- shirts with front openings.
- pants and skirts with elastic waistbands.

In the guide from the Arthritis Foundation you'll find detailed information on hundreds of self-help gadgets to order from medical product supply companies and insights from physical therapists, occupational therapists, nurses, social workers, and people with arthritis themselves. You and your parent will both want to check it out. For information on the book you can either call your local chapter of the Arthritis Foundation or call or write the national office: Arthritis Foundation, P.O. Box 19000, Atlanta, GA 30326, (404) 872-7100.

51

Disabled: Etiquette and Common Sense

Everyone is too old for something, but no one is too old for everything.
—Anonymous

If your parent has some sort of disability, she's probably learned how to deal with it from day to day. Have you? Or are you awkward around her when she has trouble walking, hearing, or seeing? There are some simple rules of "etiquette" that will help you treat her more thoughtfully. They can be especially helpful if you don't see her very often or if you have relatives who visit only occasionally and might need a briefing on their own behavior.

If She's in a Wheelchair

- Don't lean on the wheelchair too much. It's like part of her "personal space," so leaning on it all the time is sort of like leaning on her.
- Sit in a chair if you're going to talk to your parent for more than a few minutes. You can be eye-to-eye that way, and she doesn't have to crane her neck to look up at you.

- Resist the temptation to pat her on the head or shoulder. Nobody likes to be patted like a child or a dog.

If She Uses a Cane, Crutches, or a Walker

- Never offer to take her cane the way you would offer to take an umbrella or a coat unless she asks you to take it and put it away for her. She'll probably feel safer having it within reach.
- Offer to carry packages, a sweater, or anything that could be tough to handle along with a cane, crutches, or a walker. Your parent might like to carry a lightweight backpack or a hip pack because it's out of the way, but let her carry her own things. Buy her one and let her give it a try.

If He Has Hearing Problems

- Speak slowly. Get your hands away from your mouth. Stand in the light so he can watch your expressions and movements. Don't shout. Instead, speak in a low pitch—it's much easier to hear than a high-pitched voice. Be willing to repeat yourself. To get his attention, it's okay to gently tap him on the shoulder or wave your hand.
- It might be especially hard for him to hear when the whole family is gathered. Keep in

mind that a hearing aid magnifies all the noise in the room—even the roar of little kids, the TV, the clanking dishes. It can sound like a confusing racket. Don't be surprised if you see him turning OFF the hearing aid in a crowd! If you want to talk to him at a big family gathering, go off from the group for a little one-on-one.

If She Has Vision Problems

- Remind family and friends to identify themselves when they walk up to your parent. Don't make her sit for a minute or two of the conversation trying to figure out who is talking to her.
- Use a normal voice. You'd be surprised how many people shout at blind individuals.
- People always panic if they say, "See you later," to a person with severe vision problems. Don't get embarrassed if you or someone else says this to your parent. Everybody can just relax.
- When offering her a seat, put her hand on the back or arm of the chair.

If She Has Speech Problems

- Don't pretend to understand her when you really can't. It's unfair. Be encouraging; ask her to repeat. Repeat back to her what you think she said. If you think she said, "Did you enjoy church Sunday?" you can answer back with, "Yes, church Sunday was nice; the children put on a skit," instead of just "yes." Otherwise the two of you could go on forever having two completely different conversations.

• Be patient. Stroke victims often speak very, very slowly. You'll be tempted to finish every sentence. The problem is, you don't always know how she wanted her sentence to finish! Speech problems often make older people feel undignified. Listening to her with patience and love will give her back some of that dignity.

52 Stroke: Saving the Self

Giving up is the ultimate tragedy.
—*Robert J. Donovan*

In the movie *Look Who's Talking,* the voice of Bruce Willis provides us with a window into the thoughts of a baby learning what it means to be a human. This kid has the reasoning of an adult and the ability of an infant.

In a way, stroke victims are like that. The mind may know what's going on, but it can't seem to tell the body what to do about it.

Most strokes occur when a blood clot gets wedged into an artery too thin to let it pass or when a blood vessel bursts, causing a hemorrhage inside the brain. In either case, the part of the brain fed by that artery starves from lack of oxygen and nutrients, and those brain cells get damaged or die.

The effects of a stroke depend on the functions performed by the part of the brain fed by the damaged artery. A stroke on the left side of the brain (which controls the right side of the body) can impair muscle movement and feeling in the right side of the victim's body as well as cause speech and memory problems. A right-sided stroke can mess up the victim's muscle control and feeling on the left side of the body and impair space and distance perception.

Unlike most other cells, brain cells don't regenerate. To make up for this, the brain is very adaptive, remolding its ways of doing things so that other cells can take over the job of those damaged from the stroke. The brain has to relearn whatever was stored in the damaged cells—language, arithmetic, space perception, body control, etc.

This rehabilitation process can be long and hard and humiliating. Here are a few simple gestures you can make to relieve some of the frustration.

Get Going Start rehabilitation as soon as your parent is medically stable. Progress comes through work, and hope comes through evidence of progress. Also, if a stroke victim stays inactive, he runs the risk of bed sores and infections, pneumonia, muscle breakdown, blood clotting, and all sorts of nasty things sure to make a bad situation worse.

Save the Self A stroke is a devastating blow to the self-image. Imagine spending your whole life providing for others and then waking up to find you can't even control your own bladder. That's why the most pressing need is to relearn basic self-care skills: feeding, toileting, bathing, grooming, and dressing. Make them priorities.

Show Empathy To understand a small part of the frustration and helplessness your parent feels, try performing everyday tasks with one hand.

Shave; brush your teeth; button a shirt; fasten a bra; put on socks and shoes. Write a letter with your left hand if you're right-handed.

Choose Sides   If he's disabled on one side of his body, seat yourself on his good side. Otherwise, you may be just a garbled blur.

Talk Grown Up   A stroke doesn't lower a person's intelligence. Even if your parent can't speak, he probably understands you loud and clear. Speak to him as an adult.